Further Poems

By Oliver Herschel

Resemblance to any person, living or dead, is entirely coincidental.

Copyright © O. Herschel 2018

Dedicated to:

Those who support me,
and those who inspire me.

Without either, I wouldn't have had
this much courage.

Thank you.

Contained Within

1. The First Poem is a Sad One - 1
2. Dr. Frankenstein - 3
3. On the Eve of My Twentieth - 5
4. Removal and Parrish - 7
5. Under Any Other Name - 10
6. An Epistle for the Devil's Wife - 13
7. In Spirit and Sanctuary - 16
8. Patroklos - 19
9. Regarding the Shadow in front of Picasso - 21
10. Sweet Mother - 23
11. From One Lover - 26
12. The King's Guillotine - 28
13. February in Spring - 32
14. Elegy for Drowning - 35
15. The Mural on the Ceiling and the Fear of Light - 37
16. Pale Northern Lover - 40
17. Enlight - 42
18. Open Hands of Kings and Gods - 44
19. February Twenty Third - 47
20. Schoolboy - 48
21. Youth - 52
22. Birds and Men - 53
23. February Twenty Fifth - 56
24. The Poet is a Coward - 57
25. Elegy of Mulch - 59

26. A Servant to His Own Master – 61
27. Medusa – 67
28. He Was Villain – 71
29. Fictional Fatal Flaw – 73
30. Old Desert City Lights – 75
31. Spinning Wheel – 78
32. 化け物 (Monster) – 80
33. March Sixth – 83
34. Gaia – 86
35. Touch – 88
36. March Seventh – 91
37. Through His Teeth – 93
38. To Whom It May Concern – 94
39. Widow – 96
40. Under a Magnolia Tree – 97
41. Alcibiades – 100
42. Arrows in Pale Marble – 103
43. Syntax – 106
44. Flounder – 108
45. Venus/Kama/Ishtar – 109
46. ゲームの狐 (Fox's Game) - 110

Acknowledgements

The First Poem is a Sad One

I think of the two of us
Adrift out, perhaps beneath a sea
My boat is starting to rust
And your blood riddled with disease

I think of a sudden crash
The lightning strikes into the waves
And I hold back, my tongue to lash
You struggle to stand in underwater caves

From far beyond, don't die in my ears
The things that guide you now are fears
And though I recoil now from your screams
You smile again within my dreams

You now in light, in sickness
And I in darkness, in health
Perhaps the best comes with social finesse
And abandonment of platonic wealth

I am not worth any tears I cause you
Nor should you cause any of mine
Forgive any years wasted through
The time we spent chasing sublime.

Dr. Frankenstein

I despise your attempts of science
Explain me with your reason and doubt
For I, to be your hypothesis, is a silence
And to become words on a page, worth a bout

Of rage at this utter dehumanization
You take my tongue and tear it out
My words are but bastardization
To demoralize your findings, you shout

Please realize, I was never an experiment
And people like me have committed no crime
You see a question in my existence
And deny to comply to a sense of rhyme

The reason you have sought us to this end
I know where your interest lies
You wish to make them apprehend
And fear what may live within my eyes.

On the Eve of My Twentieth

I've a ton on my tongue
And dirt knit into the skin of my knees
In my brain a bass boosted and pounding
At the hollow of my eardrums

I've grown conscious of the fallacies
That rest within my body
Of the twisting feeling in my chest
My heart that's not my heart
And the twisting throbbing of fear
That I know is my brain lying to me.

If I found myself the serpent or tree
Would you be to me Eve

Or Lilith and take what I offer?
If I found myself a bull or his son
Expectations are your sword to me
To slaughter for the infidelity
And for the savagery he bred into me.

My tongue laden with lead
And voice cracked through pleasantry
The back be the only powerful thing
And eyes upon it alight in these
Words and pedantry grasping to a will
The death of man and man to hell.

The demons trace along their steps
And to bear the Devil's kiss amiss
For if I am to be the Serpent in Eden
And the Kingdom I rule proclaimed abandoned
The soldiers I govern are men like me
And men alone are the most fearsome thing.

Removal and Parrish

An old dog snarled at you
Hair raised in its fear
Your sense indecent, oppressive
The old dog snapped its teeth

You claim to have none
No power, no fear, no inferiority
It's ignorance or arrogance that propels you
Over the hills of bodies bowed
Even in death they worship you

A sword-like tongue, you claim
A benevolent god to be
A humble man whose hubris
Even the gods can see

A vagrant throat, you be

Blind to the power of words

These people melt at your feet

With desperate hands and desperate mouths

They taste the dust of your shoes

And crave the salt of your lips

Turn to me now, tell me

The realm of your control

You see nothing, but dirt

You miss the mountains and seas

So whisper to me now

And know that these words are true

The people who cling to you, you claim

Weakness rules their veins

I challenge you this,

The people you hate, who follow you

They have the power to kill, repent

For if I am Evil, then you are Idol
And the masses that fall to you
Abide in me.

Under Any Other Name

Born from rubble, and steeped in greed
I bear a wealthier man's pride
Head in a lie, and vibrant silence
Becoming my own adversary

Against my reflection, I'll raise my blade
And watch him do the same
An eye for an eye
Since ancient times, stricken
Both by blow and words

Born from silence, and bred in media
My adversary sits on my bed
With him I'll lie, and bleed, and fight
Until one of us is dead

He wishes not my destruction
I know this; he told me
But to me he is everything
I was not born for, as, or to be
From his fingers bleed diamonds
From my own, slate

The words he grows for me
Belong in the mouth of a wiser man
Belong in the mouth of a God
And yet he wills me

"Speak, here, young King.
You've got Evil under your fingernails
And Cunning in your teeth.
The crowds, they part, young King.
A Red Sea before you
Absent ears eager for order.

"It's chaos you bring, young King.
With hungry mouths and throats
Your people thrive in it.
Do you doubt me, young King?
Bare me your throat
And see if I reach."

An Epistle for the Devil's Wife

Hands are like claws

Reaching through and into with heavenly voice

Flight, the movement within

Chest turns upwards and grasps

Higher still, it can be felt

Your song stuck into my skull

A lullaby and a sonnet

A serenade rattling within my brain

The echoes of your voice

Like a nymph in my ear

You sing of being a siren

And the feeling within my chest knows it is true

For I am drawn forth and into the past
Where you, at your prime,
Cry out in soprano
And I, in silence,
Can only grasp at the waves

In my head, your voice is red
Your song, your melodies
You sing of being the Devil
I understand, for I do too
And I realize those words have always belonged to you

Echoing Plato, calling me a liar
I fault you for it not
For your songs call me dead
And within I have always been that much

The nymph in my ear

Became the nymph in my throat
And my fingers too as your words sear
Into my skin and the only thing I know
Are death, beauty, and love

I'm sure once ago
You did not make my heart sway so
But here we are, sweet siren
Your song bids me to stone.

In Spirit and Sanctuary

Your fingers are like your brother's

They're shy yet wander

And wonder with hesitance –

Is it safe to touch?

Your lips quiver

In a fear like his

So cautious to taste skin

And you ask with whispers concealing your lips

–

Is it safe to kiss?

Breathe, he bids it

The way you hold it in is injustice

For you, he fears

A mirrored fate the Fates align

A crown of snakes
You both had worn
Through that alertness to my tune
You turn away and hide your shame
But shaking fingers stitch my name

You will not learn from his mistakes
And dye your dress in red
For him it was a handkerchief, but you
You submerge in it

You had watched him tied up and burned
When they saw the traces of my tongue
Did your eyes light up seeing the shadows
Twist and bundle to my form

Were you so enraptured and longing

Hands reaching through the flames

Skin broiling to marked pox

And wistful eyes falling to me

That you failed to notice the fire

Being passed to you

Oh, but I did love you

While it lasted, just like him

The fire claimed to clean your souls

But left you smoke and ash

Do I now linger by your pyre

With cloudy eyes waiting

For either you or your brother

To rise from this dust?

But ignore me, my old loves

This mourning is my fallacy

And to your deaths, you're owed sympathy

So take my blood instead.

Patroklos

With a culture such as this

Do not criticize the virgin

For thinking of scratches on skin

Of his back to the dirt

Of painful but lustful tears and screams

Bred such as these, in these homes

Each same but mirrored

Stairs on right, now on left

Our beds would be flush

And between this wall, and through this wall

He may feel the heat of your lips

Does your longing span to these?

Through the stars and heavens and back to Earth

Where he has been laid to the river
And his body in Lethe forgotten
And your hands to Styx in fame.

See now, through his eyes,
You shine like a god in the moonlight
You've always been the beautiful one
And in your rage, your strength
To tear through the ones
Who may take the face you wear to his
And excuse his broken form.

Regarding the Shadow in front of Picasso

"I'm easily charmed,"

I say, back straight, and eyes forward.

He smells of cigarettes and aftershave.

"Why do you say that?"

He bids my eyes, so I look.

His jacket undone and chin stubbled.

"I'm a poet,"

I tell him.

"What else should I be?"

"Wise," says he, a smirk defacing lips

"Shouldn't you know the world we're in?"

He seems amused by the laugh I give
Letting my weight shift back, to my heel
The crow before us raises its head
And gives out a guttural cry.

"A poet," I reply, turning away
"is never wise. What a thought –
I only need to have words
That I can say
To reflect on the days
Past and to come and the images of life."

And a moment of silence passes between us.

"A poet is a poet,
Not a philosopher."

Sweet Mother

There is no life in Mother's womb
But still two hearts beat
In synch in tune

She hates the heavy weight
That clings to her legs
And to her ribs
So when she raises her arms
She sees white skin

There is no food on Mother's plate
And though her arms shake
Her muscles plead, she ignores

Her mind is on her tongue
She thinks it sexual while
She starves the meat from her bones
And bruises them
On the walls of her self-begotten cage

There is no life in Mother's eyes
She breathes and she walks
But she cannot feel

Does she smother you
While you sleep, dear son?
Does she give the food to you?
You stand outside her cage
And you feel her weakness
In your arms and legs

There is no water in Mother's cup
And there is none in yours

Two who drink of sex and storm
>   Mouths open fangs wide
>   And leaking with a blood
>   That looks the same as mine.

From One Lover

Oh, my sweet Sigyn
With your hand you carry this
The sorrow of my crucified and wretched soul
A blessed and gentle touch
To caress my cheek and fill me
My soul with warmth and life
To your light and love

Oh, my sweet bride
In your heart and lips you wear fidelity
Your abrasive shade of red
And to that red, to my skin
The marks of your kiss within my wrists
Your faith and peace too rich
To counter my made-evil

Your pain for me, sweet Sigyn
Reminds of my deeds
Dig into my skin and soul
Your tears burn worse than the poison
And I'd bid you, leave me
But stay, stay by this altar
To truly die would be to be left alone.

The King's Guillotine

Mountain king, you're faded to the ashes
That remain of your home and rubble
Lies strewn along this canyon floor
Admonishments with the strike of your blade
Poor to the throat and hark to the living
The dead make your kingdom
And your kingdom is the land

Mountain king, your throat to the altar
And the altar hangs the blade
The God we appease is wise
And he knows why you live and why you die
In our ears, he whispers your truth
As a man in white mask ascends
Your executioner takes the rope

And we are at our edge

Mountain king, I cared for you
For the time you allotted me
Let your gaze fall to me at last
For I am within the crowd
You can ignore their shouts and focus
I hope you remember my name
Our God is benevolent, but
He would not spare your soul

Mountain king, make of me your final wish
Before these masked devils feast of your sin
Perhaps I have the power to set you free
With a curse and with a kiss
I could make you an Iron king
But Mountain king you betray me
With your eyes to the ground and the blade
Hanged so solemn to your neck

Mountain king, I see in your eyes

Absolution to our God's decree

Your sin, you think, is thick in your blood

And our God would claim it so

You think there's no hope

He would then agree

And don a mask to strike you

Is this reverence to him?

Is this your transcendence?

Mountain king, you do not look to the crowd

And you lay down your sword

Fall to your knees and our God chants it

It is time for a climax and demise

And I had wished it to not come to this

But among this masked crowd

There is no choice for me

They are all bloodthirsty

They don't remember who you used to be

Mountain king, our time here is done

Our God has retreated back

Into the trees, and the trees close around him

Their masks are disposed, and their faces are blank

Your blood on the rock

Sin would have left a bigger stain.

February in Spring

Is it raining?

No, but the sidewalk is wet

And the ground is covered in mud

And smells like the deep parts of the forest

The parts where the animals shit

Is it raining?

No, but I wish it was

Perhaps the walls would be silent

And against the window it would hit

And I'd have something to drown

This ache in my throat with

It is raining?

No, but it was, at a point

And the sky is grey like it might
So it may, sometime today
But at this moment, it is not.

Why should it rain?
I think we all need it
The air is thick and swampy
And this refrain is making something
Wind up in my chest

Heaven, I can tell you need to release
Perhaps hear it in my dreams
But you wake me in the night
And affect my days in such this way

Heaven, do so tonight
And serenade my slumber
With the sounds of falling
Of striking the glass and roof

Let me have, at least, this.

Elegy for Drowning

A deep blue wrapped like a blanket
The sun a spotlight somewhere high
Above the water and within it
And it's dark but it's vibrant and warm

The water feels like air
And eyes like frog's fixed
Floating and drifting deeper
It's dark but it's loving for once

See nothing but that light
And it's yellow, and hot against skin
That cannot, for once, feel it
It's dark but it feels like home

And being surfaced from that world
Shaking and choking
On the toxic air and monochrome world
Missing the floating and falling and peace.

The Mural on the Ceiling and the Fear of Light

God gave me this sadness

Pieced it all, stringed it all together

Painted it up on the ceiling

The story of a life

Of blurry eyes and dolls in windows

Choirs, pianos, and church bells

Wrapped up as one and into one

Scraping metal against the pavement

And violins ringing in my ears

God gave me this sadness

Maybe thinking I would become an Atlas

Maybe thinking I would crumble beneath

Putting these knives in my hands

A quiet and godly voice over my shoulder

Into my ear a whisper

That everything is alright

And that any action I take will show my might

God gave me this sadness

Crammed it down my throat

Put me in front of a mirror

And told me to hate it

And to fear it

To shield my eyes from the blaring lights

And when I hate it

And fear it

A chortle.

God gave me this sadness

And mocked me for it

You ask me if I pray when I feel it?

The God you love gave it

So I keep it

And with line after line

Verse after verse

And stanzas abound

I bury it within itself

And within the words it creates

Pale Northern Lover

At the behest of my professor

O what an odd thing you must be
To one who does not know you
Like a lover, your form on the ground
A caress and kiss, you send to me
One whom the North Wind carries
You and I in a single gasp
I know you as a husband
Your movement, scent, and touch

O what good you give them love
They melt to you, craving your satisfaction
A toy to them, my love, and they hold you
In one night of passion, but grow weary
Let me lie with you, I who am familiar

With your bite and hate and nails
Let me lie with you, without them
And show me your brand of love.

Enlight

What have you got beside these trembling lips

Unwashed and impure fingertips

Sloughing the masses of possession

Milking the greedy of inhibition

Oh but you're wise, we know it

Familiar as you are with the ghosts

The wights and ghouls that haunt the streets

Did they bear you? You move like one

Twisted apart with black sheets

The shadows are your silence

And your silence are their nightmares

How they fear you! They bemoan

A fire at the twist of your wrists

They lose but you win
Oh, our hero, where is the fault in that?

Pearls you've gained and earned
Through the harshness of your trade
Now spurn! Reject their claim
It's yours, has been
Since your eyes fell upon it
Since your fingers grasped it

Dare we say it, but you have become
That to which we aspire
In our sleep you creep
With soft-soled shoes
Into the shadows of your forbearers
Becoming one with it
And causing another man grief

Open Hands of Kings and Gods

He is You, who fails to entomb me
Oh how You shake, dear heart
You and Your marriage bed, a lie
Whispered into the night
Like a savage man to a flame

You're reverent, but fearful
In Your hands, I can feel it
Aching for sublimity but
Trapped in liminality

Bare the pieces of You that cause You pain
How boorish the blessings You bring
To outstretched arms and bony wrists

Finding justice and peace within it

Oh, but what do You bring?
Your heart and hand aches for nothing
The stream from Your lips, I know them
All lies, as though it is Your passion

Oh, but do You know me, dear heart?
I who capture and ensnare
The hearts of immortals and greats
Within my mind
Of my own right and claim
Of an imagined earth

Believe You me that this land
My own, to me, a young king
So open and wide and flourishing
It does not belong to You
And never will, even in Your lies

Your dreams, my dear heart
They're amusing, and more
You speak as though this land
Is already Yours

How foolish and naïve
Your brow may strain for nobility
With not a drop in Your blood
And Your lips, they claim
Through my throat and skin
All I own is passed to You

How forward a claim, dear heart
When You, I maintain for my own
A puppet for desire and pain
While I will remain unknown to You.

February Twenty Third

"Do I love you?

Do I love you?"

Your words ring like a plea

A silent call for aid

But it is a question

To which the answer is unknown

To all but you

Please tell me, for now I wish to know

Does your heart beat

Fast or slow when you see me?

Does your breath hitch?

Have you made the decision

To give your time to me?

Do you love me?

I do not know.

Schoolboy

Oh but call me a young fool

I'll yearn and ache for the unattainable

I'll dream and read of kings

Seated up on their thrones,

But their hearts aching for someone

And that honor falling to me

To a surrogate of me

Who knows my shape and manner

Who can love this man for me

Oh but aching remains in devouring

My gentle and tender soul

Resting within these pages and taking

Capturing the heat in my cheeks

As I read and imagine myself

In the arms of the king

Oh but I am a young fool
With the dreams of a schoolboy
Who wishes to be taken far away
And treasured and cared for
To be held and kissed and yearned for

My anxiety comes from reality
In that I cannot speak
Could not reach for any who would be my king
Ignore the rocks in my throat
That forbid my speech
Or the crow that borrows my eyes
To draw them to any but him

Oh I've been imagining a king
Like a younger me curled up in blankets
Smile wide and eyes to the future

With no fear of mortality
And the short life of a poet
This king, you see
His hands cover me
And he is warm who holds me

Would he like tea, as I do?
Would he want me to lie
Back to the wall and use my voice
And weave him little stories?
Oh but I imagine him often
And beside me he is
There to take my hand and lead me
Toward the fear and terror of reality

Oh future king of mine
I bid you, please come to me
And pronounce me a lover
For I know not how to walk this path

And I know not how to approach you

Oh future king of mine
I bid you, come quick
Take my frozen heart into your burning hands
And cure me of my diseases

I pray, you know me
I pray, you come
Else I'll be alone for ever
Else my heart will plague my mind
And turn it to rot

Youth

Whether alone or at your behest
I find myself hating the sun
The way it beats down
And comes through the window
Waking me in the morning
What right does that blasted thing have?
To bake my skin and leave me blistered
To disrupt the night and give the world reason
A cause for noise and movement
Oh, why don't we all relax for once?
Give this all a pause
And let me sleep in peace

Birds and Men

Lover, are you a raven or a crow?

Dressed in black

So sleek and beautiful

With a strong shout and wide wings

Oh, but so mischievous

Father, am I shouting into the emptiness?

I hear no cries in reply

And when aid is needed, nothing comes

Alone, alone I climb

To the peak, and define myself

And the emptiness will stare back

Mother, are you sharpening your claw?

Remember not the pain you cause me

Or the scars you've left on my skin
Where your beak snaps
Plume bristles with pride
But you've skin and that
Is what disturbs me

Lover, do you feel the light?
Oh how warm it is
How it filters through these trees
Feeling like a summer breeze
Both enthralled by its simple magic

Father, why am I not satisfied?
To you I cry for guidance
But on the other side of this screen
Is there nothing?
Good Father, Reverend of the Christian God
Are you apart of the emptiness too?

Mother, can you feel the darkness closing?
Ask after me as you do
Perhaps it is care
But I know you better
Oh I know talons and feathers
And the trenches dug into me

Lover, will you stay the night?
How cold it is becoming
With shaking limbs, I bid you
I wish only for these things
To hold and be held by you

February Twenty Fifth

I believe I am worthy
To be loved by myself
And others

To look in the mirror
And smile and be happy
And love the smile I see

I believe I am worthy
That who I am is enough
And what I know is enough

I believe I am enough
And that I deserve
To be happy.

The Poet is a Coward

Have you seen his arms?
They're like toothpicks
But his waist tucks into a pleasant curve
And the bones of his wrists
They can be seen through his skin
But you could fit a fist around his neck

Brother dearest, your hips are wide
And you've too much on your thighs
But you've gotten smaller, congrats
Brother dearest, you haven't eaten for hours?
Feel yourself thinning, congrats

Have you seen his ankles?
So delicate, they'd break if
You touch them in the slightest

But his stomach groans
That means he's doing well

Brother dearest you've got your mind
Thinking good thoughts like
What's wrong with skipping the meal?
You don't need it
And you fear what it might do
Brother dearest are you a coward?
Fearing the smallest bit of weight
You call yourself a man?

Oh but you have no strength
No muscles to your arms
Is it because, good brother dearest
You fear the women who bemoan
The slightest meat on your bone
What they say? How they twist you!
Yearning for a warm meal
But a drink will do just fine.

Elegy of Mulch

How it brings me into the past
Fills me with new life
And sinks me to my knees

Oh bury me in this
This rich dark soil
Fresh and soft, with scent

That sends me to the gardens
Of the past I'd tried to grow
Of tomato vines and dragon bells

These leaves I feel them
Between my fingers, on my skin
So thick and rough

But fills my throat and mind
With the memories of a boy
Knelt in the grass beside a flowerbed

Hands covered in dirt
With a bright shining grin
And a deep breath.

A Servant to His Own Master

Eyes to the sun

I begin to feel worthy

Perhaps even holy

And I wonder where this preoccupation

Was created from

A celestial form such as this

Washing over pallid skin

Bathing it, cleansing it

Was this truly what was needed?

Eyes to the moon

And weak at the knees

The stars to their Queen

And Terra claiming.

Their shapes and forms
Dance in the twilight
In the brush fires
That burn up in the heavens
In blues and greens and purples
A calming and claiming Aurora.

Oh and in this light
I feel as though I've regained something
That was once lost to me
Within me, it fades
But it burns and even more now
Can I feel it
Hollow or full? Perhaps both
Trampling over the other
And climbing up into my throat.

Out here, could I touch the horizon
Could I bathe in this night

The sky that closes overtop me
And holds me in its arms
Like some forbidden
Mistress, but lips of starlight
And eyes alight like the moon
And these moonbeams cover me
Encasing and entombing me in this
Darkness but so bright and beautiful!

She's aflame in this starlight
And she lives within it
Lost to my weary, mortal hands
But she becomes the divinity
I had prayed to and belonged to
Oh move these lips in prayer
Beautiful twilight above!
These trees are your fingers
And the light I'd feared your love.

On my knees, let me plead

I've lost my strength and wish

With what I have left,

Remaining within me

I make vow, oath, and pledge.

Let you be my divinity

The Mistress in this night

To you I will give! All

That remains within this infertile ground.

Take my youth

Take my tongue

Take my fingers or arms or lungs

I need them not.

Already, I have lived a hollow life

And without the sight of this light

I fear it to return

Oh should I have remained in fear of you?

In fear of this daze you've set upon me?
Remove your spell from my eyes
Sweet Mistress, let me see for myself
If this night is full of the colors
And beauty you promised
Everything you've shown
My reputation with deities is not good
So I will suspect a lie from you
But give me, Sweet Mistress
The benefit of the doubt.

Let me see these colors
With my own eyes
And let me judge it
In fairness and truth
Enraptured though I had been,
It was pain!
So let me, in my health again
With no spell beset on me

Look on thy night.

Medusa

Oh scream! I bid you!
Let out your fear and rage
Seep your anger into his blood
And claw with your fingers to his ribs
Oh bleed! Make him bleed!
He's turned you to this
And exists for the
Dying light

Taste it
Why don't you?
Lick your fingers clean
Of the gore he bore upon you
Lover fair, you owe them all nothing
You owe them what you owe me

You owe me a beating

For the pain that

I caused

To you

Once so divine

Among all the others

My loving you made you a

Beast so foul none can look beyond

None will look beyond your eyes

None can and we both know

Why that is and it's

My fault

I know

How I feel this

Regret and pain for my

Actions, her reactions that

Cast you to this form, you were

Once divine, more beautiful

Than Aphrodite in face

In form and in

Bearing

Yes, this

Is something I

Should ask for peace

From you for me as I saw

You as more, and more I saw

Than she had wrought

Upon you here

This form

Do you

Think it so ugly

That you hide from the

Light in that dwelling of darkness

Do you think it so crude

That you keep

It from

Me, the

One who gave

It to you, through my

Misgivings and deeds, direct

That hate and anger to me, lover fair

I deserve it more than they.

Oh if I send a son

Would you be

Appeased?

He Was Villain

Darling heart, could you bear me?
I have lied and stolen and cheated
My words have been manipulation
On the ones I should love and honor
On the ones you're most loyal to

My actions to you, darling heart
Were nigh unforgivable that night
My actions to you, sweet bride
You who have done things
That I should have followed suit

Myself, so shrewd, how was it
That I got you and you me?
Money from the most calculating

The one who sets things in order
And watches them fall in place

I worry you feared me
Nor were you at fault
For the things I said and did
I used you, you were a pawn
In a higher plan that was worth nothing
In my chest, I am heavy.

Inescapable, such deplorable anguish
Given to you and returned to me
Without cause, without reason
The wrong I've done to you
Like Cain cycle back
I'll choke on my silver tongue
Because of the pain in your heart.

Fictional Fatal Flaw

In my head

You live solely in my head

Don't you?

You don't care if I'm alone

In outside life

Because I return to you

Promising vibrancy

Vitality and veniality

To throat and chest and head

You only want me to return

When I'm lonely

Or when I feel you

And oh god how I feel you
Leave me please
Leave me to sanity

Leave me to a sanctuary
I wish not to feel your hands
When there's nothing

Why must you torment me so?
Were you those voices too?
That taunted in my ear every failure?

Good god how I feel you
Now, even now, especially now
I don't want to

How cruel you can be
I want nothing
Not you.

Old Desert City Lights

You've got a light

For an old friend?

Come share it and lay down your head

We're both lost here,

And endlessly hoping

For something to come of everything

Every loose end in life

Must have a meaning

Set up and pay off

But reality ain't that nice

You got your head down

Drift quick to sleep

Keep heart, I'll keep watch
And tell you when the lights turn
Red to green, yellow and blue
When we can go
And run ourselves
In this worn out car
Right off a cliff

You know the kind, I don't
You know the tastes and sounds
The blazing colors of neon
On that strip of road I hate
Depravity I sneer at and you laugh

Boy, you asked me back then,
You think you're better than this town?
You're like them,
The heat of your skin and the way
You crave and cheat and devour

But you were right back then
>   And it's still true
>   You're harsh on me
>   And I'm harsh on you.

Spinning Wheel

You're poison, and it frightens me
That you're so close
And in the night I could prick myself on you
Condemn myself to the fate I love
You're poison and you're beautiful
But aren't all lovely things?

You give something to this
The white and tan emptiness
Of this room you give your color
Your life, in a way I never could
Thrive, thrive I'll give you sunlight
Make piece with this heat and flourish
I'll hope for you to give me peace
But what will you think of me?

Can you, and will you

My next question be

Feel and know you're here

To be loved and kept and keep

Me alive in the darkness of night

And the chill of winter, despite you

Despite your toxins, despite it all

But will you live for me?

It's selfish, so very

But I cannot help but ask

To muse on you as the sun slips through

The clouds that blot out the sky in white

And grey and black but it's come through

And shines on you and I wonder

I cannot help it

I feel at peace with you

But how long can I keep something living?

化け物

You see a marionette dance

Bathed in shadows with jointed limbs

She moves and moves

Her jaw clacks to the song

The music and the beat

Ask yourself any number of thing

I will be behind to tell you

To put you on your feet

And let you know the secrets

What stands behind her?

Back where we cannot see?

What hastens her step

Apart from the song

What forces her to dance?

You see a marionette

She stands tall, upright

Greets you and offers you solace

But what voice is this

With which she speaks?

What language does she use?

How did she learn it?

Why is it this puppet

A poppet

Why does she sound like you?

Look like you?

And when you dance,

She dances, and when she dances

You feel as if your feet bleed

I will dance with you and you with me

I will sing to you and you to me

Keep moving and moving

And maybe the man who made her

Won't notice the difference.

March Sixth

I will keep walking

Past these scourges and flames

Through the canyons I've built

And the valleys I've dug

I will persist

I will keep going

Even if my legs crumble

And my lungs turn to dust

Or my brain turns to poison

I will overcome

I will keep living

Despite the tide of night

When the moon pulls my soul

And twists into my head
I will survive

I will keep walking
When the crowds pile up
And the ground falls out beneath me
And the sands of time lap at my feet
I will go on

I will persevere
And block out all the words
My mind shouts at me
Voice like a bark, day and night
I will live

I will continue
Because that is my power
That is the strength I have
My way to make my statement

I will live.

Gaia

To lend it all

Strength and dreams and hope

Prayers and faith

To the deserving one

In the light of Helios

Feeling as though your arms

Coming around me, embracing me

Are the mountains

And the trees

And even the buildings of man

Buildings built by your grace

Of your grace

Provider, none of this without you

So let me lie down

Onto your rolling blankets of green

The nurturing you offer

Given to me, simply to me

And I am cleaned

Freed, in your spring

As once again you come alive

Choke in my throat, this prayer

A psalm of joy

Whispered to the Earth

To the dirt

And to you

Sweet Mother who gives to me

My strength

And to whom I return it

And to whom I will return.

Touch

Years back, years ago

I know you knew and felt it

Fingers to your spine

Mouths to curl around yours

And read your mind

Gloriousness and glory

In thought to thought to mine

Depravity? No, perish

Purity, as such in this

Your tears to taste

In velvet strop

And blood and blood divine

You reach and reach

With pale veined hand

Across the veil of time

So touch! O touch

Sweetest Harbinger of this

These lines that connect you and I

Though you cannot read them

And they may not persist

My message to you shall lie

Within these lines

A letter perhaps

To the ghost of a man long dead

Horseman of my poetry

I've seen every inch of you

In my mind's eye so take mine

My own reflection alongside yours

And break through the sands of time

Let youth persist for us both

And let age fear us

Let our bodies be purified by verse
Let our minds be purified by rhyme.

March Seventh

I try to keep a little thing alive

But what a task it is

To it, my mind wanders

When the sun has set around six

Starving little flower

Shriveled up in the cold

I tried to keep it alive

But my thumb is brown

As a dried up weed

Still living and yet

Spring comes not for you

Too hot too cold

Somewhere in between

Your dinner hates you

Little yellow flower

Have I hastened your pace

As you wither away

Thanks to cloud and chill

You sit at my windowsill and yet

The sun shines past those clouds and yet

You starve.

Through His Teeth

Mountain king, they're burying me in gold
Your grave is for naught
And our God says nothing
His gaze is vacant and ice

Mountain king, they paint me in gold
By the metal in your blood
And the blood in your sin
Our God looks on

Mountain king, they make my blood gold
What say you? What say you?
What liars they are
Our God is dead.

To Whom It May Concern

Think naught on it
Think nothing of it
My word is my own
And to me it is clear
A window into my mind
These rampant thoughts of mine
The way it looks, built, and feels

Too many times
I've heard from their mouths
The subject is false
Either it is God, I am God,
Or I am Icarus
But the fall is my folly

But not my folly, I laugh
As I fall, and say it's your fault

In a room of academics
I am an artist
Hesitate to call myself a poet
But hasten to embrace it
I will bear it
And in charm I will wear it
This poetry of mine

But is it?
Lean back, magnifying glass
Is it?
My friend, look closely
The trick is pressing
[Enter]

Widow

Chains, chains within me
Deep within me it overflows
Rattling and grating into the soul
Into the soul and onto the soul

Hands, hands onto me
Covering me, eight winding arms
Winding around me, a ghost's embrace
Consume the soul and devour the soul

The skin, along it
Licking and cutting with forked tongues
Forked tongues that stretch and curl
A ghost would flee in horror
Within the soul and outside the soul

Under a Magnolia Tree

The Death I knew, he loved me
How he would occupy my thoughts
And me his
And I'd wait for fingers of bone
On my wrist on my waist

He did not wait for me
I continue to wait for him
Both of us in the shadows of night
In his realm, whispering

He is one who longs for that
Which he cannot touch
While I only long for him

Hands connected, combined
Entwined, pale full flesh
And his own, like a mirror
And he spoke to me
He whispered as we two were covered
By the shadow, the veil
This good being vowed to me
And I to him
Sickness, health, life and Death

None of it would matter to us
And we'd become one of the shadows
When Time is up and Ages are done
And the Age of mankind falters
His arms would encircle me

A constant reminder that he was there
Watching, lingering, despite not speaking
And not taking – letting me drown

Watching my eyes lose their light
As my mind rotted with life
And within me my heart
Shriveled to dust

With me he thrives as a phantom does
In the shadows of the night
Accompanying the lonely
His fingers, sharp as they are
Pawing and keening at my throat
I dwell on him and pray to him

But my king ignores me.

Alcibiades

Look at him

He drowns in luxury

And lives surrounded by many

Who swim in his whims

He's got solid teeth

They close at my throat

Because I envy him

He tears me apart

Look at me

The person I am in my head

Is so wholly divorced from reality

Married to Death and fucked by Gods

This man in my head

Thriving in me, though he is
Rips me to pieces

I find myself feeling as he does
Bleeding as he does
And for him I must wait

His fingers slough old wealth
And his pride is the same as mine
Burn in it, I will
Breathe it with coal-tainted lungs

I know I lack what he owns
But still I'll wish
With lips painted in the blood of kings
And fingers in the blood of the altar
I walk a path

The light at the end of the pier

To become me.

Arrows in Pale Marble

Attest to me, an old shell

Crumbling beneath the weight of nations

With a hardened tongue

Shield my spine from this

Twenty-six daggers for the king

And a crown of snakes for the maiden

Witness my fall and rise: my martyrdom

Confess to me, your old scars

Strong arms beneath the sky

Dwarf or giant, it gleams beyond

The earth and the atmosphere, a prism

Stacked realms of existence

Heaven, Hell, Hades, Valhalla

And I will not reside with heroes

Freeze my bones, good queen.

Protest to me, these old bones
That ache with weight and pressure
You lower your eyes from Heaven's rise
And declare the actor virtuous
Sin to you, and sin to me
Deliver us now from our homes
Believe yourself chosen for Heaven's light
While I know I'm going to Hell

Pity me, you old man
I feel your eyes are burning
Along my back, these wings will rise
And their vision bathed in black
The horses will ride through the night
And within your chest, I feel it
The thrumming of music and beat of bass
Pulses and throbs of rhythm

Do you feel your melody
How it pauses as you look
Up to the sky and its haunts.

Syntax

I know not my immortality

I know my hushed tongue
My stilted phrase
And the words that cannot reach my lips

I know not my illusions

My demise upon my brain
Playing and playing so
The film crackles and breaks

I know not the tongue of my ancestors

I know the Way They spoke
But the Words trip on my Tongue

And spill Down my Chest

I know not my native voice

These phrases escape me
As they would any other
And in my brain is caught "in and on"

I know not the law of this world

Nor any of my own
These plants crumble in my fingers
And when I fall, I float past the clouds

I know not the value of mankind

Nor do I know my own
But they could be good or bad
And I would trust them with my lungs.

Flounder

You've got a funny tongue

And it's much smoother than mine

The way you speak is commendable

I admire you, I do

Your arms are funny, too

They're big and warm and strong

I bet they'd feel nice around me

Your face is rather odd

And I don't like the way it feels

When you look me in the eye

You're so goddamn sincere

What's the point of this?

Why do you dance around it?

You're lonely and need me

And I'm starved for human touch

So just kiss me, you idiot.

Venus/Kama/Ishtar

Romance belief and human emotion
The visceral pain that pierces at night

Romance red lips and hummed tones
Basic ethics and squandered theses

Romance sunset, sunrise, and noontime
Mixed drinks and milked jokes

Romance fidelity and the music it makes
The heated touch of hot-tempered youth

Romance confessions and white knuckles
Dilated pupils and hands that won't let go

Fall in love with love itself and learn the worth of life.

ゲームの狐

I would love to say

I disappeared that day

Vanished into the forests

And became someone new

It's nice to think

The faeries came

And took me away

Or I followed the rabbit too far

And never left the fairy tale

Maybe I think about what it would be like
If I did

If I were somewhere else right now

If I were someone else
If I got the adventure I craved

I remember a fox on the road
And I stopped and watched him run
But if I'd followed, left my bike behind
Would I be on an adventure?

Or simply lost?

Acknowledgements

-

Thank you, firstly, to everyone on Tumblr. You are the ones who gave me courage to share this poetry – and gave me the hubris to publish it myself. I would be in a very different headspace without you guys.

Secondly, gratitude – for she who encouraged me to write poetry again.

And lastly, a nod to my peers and professors – without whom I would lack motivation, inspiration, and education.

Printed in Great Britain
by Amazon